LIMBIC LIMBO

Dumpster Fire Poetry

Rachel Rash

Global Disruption Media LLC

Copyright © 2024 Rachel Rash

Global Disruption Media LLC
P.O. Box 4
Clarendon, Arkansas 72029
First published in e-book by Global Disruption Media LLC
This paperback edition 2024

Printed in the United States of America

All rights reserved. No part of this publication may be reproduced, stored in a retrieval system, or transmitted, in any form or by any means, electronic, mechanical, photocopying, recording or otherwise, without the prior permission of the publisher.

www.rachelrash.com

ISBN: 978-1-965083-02-4

Library of Congress Control Number: 2024923550

Cover design by Rachel Rash
Illustrations by Jane Finley
Editors: Alisha Eckersley and Lauren Hoffmann

I dedicate this collection of poetry to an amazing collection of women. To my mother, who contributed the artwork amongst these pages. To Alisha and Lauren, my incredible editors. To Hussna, the one that inspired the first of these poems as well as the last poem written in this collection. And to all the sisters that I have acquired through this journey called life. This book of poetry was forged by the dumpster fire of the 2020's, and I would not want to walk through the flames with anyone else.

CONTENTS

Title Page
Copyright
Dedication
Introduction
The Title
The Poems   2
Section I   4
Hussna - Part 1   6
Hussna - Part 2   7
*Hussna Footnotes   8
I Am Woman   10
Priestess   12
Soul Sisters   13
Livestock   14
Section II   16
Awen   17
*Awen Footnotes   18
Entropy   19
The Liminal Mist   20

Air	21
Ambedo	22
Old Ones	23
Sands of Time	24
Recycled	25
Section III	26
Rantings of My Mind	28
No One Else	29
Erode	30
You Never Know	31
Greed	32
Minutes for Sale!	33
Quicksand	34
Morphine	35
Into the Night, Again	36
Justice Served Too Late	38
The More I Ask	39
Blap, Blap	40
Section IV	42
Glue On It	44
Autonomy	45
Fire-Borne	46
Honour and Strength	47
Hanging by a Thread	48
On the Shoulders of Others	49
Section V	52

Atlas Shrugged	54
Mind Killer	55
*Mind Killer Footnote	56
Interlinked	57
*Interlinked Footnote	58
Don't Burn Me	59
*Don't Burn Me Footnote	60
Glossary	61
About The Author	62

INTRODUCTION

Thank you for picking up a copy of this book! It was a brainchild of the early 2020's. These pages contain all of the emotions and struggles from that time. Feelings which are still felt at the time of publishing. I hope that in the future, these will have passed; then, this collection of poetry will simply be a placeholder of memories. The poems are free-verse style, and are my debut collection. I have added footnotes to poems where I thought additional context would add depth. This is not a traditional format. Feel free to skip to the next page, where the next poem will be waiting for you.

When I was a child, I always wanted to be a writer. My mother and I made our own children's books. I would write the words and she would illustrate. We even investigated how to have copies published by local printing companies. We were years ahead of the self-publishing era and quickly learned that printing a small run of full color children's books would cost more than we could ever sell the copies for. Fast forward twenty years or so and now independent publishing is a reality. While this book may not be the original format and content we developed our ideas around, it is a dream come true. This book is available in multiple formats; whichever format you prefer to digest content in, I hope you enjoy. Visit my website www.rachelrash.com to stay informed and up-to-date.

Sincerely,

Rachel Rash
November 23rd, 2024

THE TITLE

You might be wondering about the title of this book. I thought long and hard about what a fitting title would be for a collection of poetry such as this. Limbic Limbo was the winner from all of the options. Limbic meaning the subconscious portion of the brain controlling one's emotions and memories. Limbo meaning an uncertain period, awaiting resolution. The subtitle Dumpster Fire Poetry is an allegory to the time in which these poems were written in.

THE POEMS

SECTION I

The Feminine

HUSSNA - PART 1

Our world is dissolving in chaos,
My soul is heavy and exhausted.

My heart is full of broken despair,
There has been too much to repair.

The world you were born to,
Is right now a memory,
Nothing so far can compare,
And I pray for better days too,
That the present become a memory,
Or be just a nightmare.

I wish for you to be in school,
And wear whatever you think is cool.

My day is your night, your night my day,
May your night's shadow turn into a sun ray.

HUSSNA - PART 2

Our world is still dissolving in chaos,
My soul is even heavier and more exhausted.

My heart is still broken, for you, for the world,
And nothing has been able to repair it.

Now, you're engaged to be someone's wife,
When you should be worrying about high school,
Maybe this is your salvation from the long night,
Maybe this is how you go back to school,
When you emerge from this darkness,
You'll be in a new country, and be a new wife.

All I wanted, was for you to go back to school,
To be able to wear what you thought was cool.

My day is your night, your night my day,
May your night's shadow turn into a sun ray.

*HUSSNA FOOTNOTES

The ending phrase in both poems is not just a metaphor, but a reference to the time difference between Hussna and myself.

Hussna - Part 1:
This is the poem that began this collection of poetry. Hussna is a young girl living in Afghanistan. When the country fell back into the hands of the Taliban, she had to stop going to school. It has been over three years and the situation for girls, and women, has only gotten worse. She is the youngest of an entire family of highly-educated women. Most are doctors and lawyers. Family members have bought her books to study in secret at home, but her future remains uncertain. As are many futures across the economically struggling country where women make up 49.5% of the total population.

Hussna - Part 2:

Part 2 was written three years after the first Hussna poem. Now, a young woman, Hussna is engaged to be married. Her betrothed lives outside of Afghanistan, which could be her saving grace to leave the country and return to the freedoms she previously knew. This could also mean returning to her studies. However, due to her young age, they will not be married for several years. On one hand, this is good because she is still young. On the other hand, she cannot leave Afghanistan until they are married. For now, she will have to endure for a while longer. And she will miss the rest of her teenage years. Once she can go freely in public again, or have her voice be heard, she will be someone's wife.

I AM WOMAN

The question has been asked,
And quite a lot lately,
What it means to be a woman.
Does it mean hormones, chromosomes,
Body parts, or an amalgamation?
It has even been suggested,
And by a fellow woman no less,
That women are weaker than men,
Created by God that way!
The very thought and audacity!

I abhor this thought, detest it even,
For if by Biblical commentary,
We shall view and debate this question,
Then woman would have never come to be,
Had Adam not been lonely,
Without companion helpless,
So might we suggest that God took pity,
Giving Adam a partner from his own body,
And if from himself she came,
How dare he call her weak.

Through birth pangs, millenia after millenia,
Women have carried and borne,
We stand on the shoulders,
Of the women that came before us,
Such a mix of pain and joy,
That is what it means to be a woman,
Willing to die to save others,
Or live to protect and shelter,
We are our sovereign selves,
Needing no permission from any man.

I am woman, we are woman,
The most bittersweet thing,
So in conclusion, I say this once again,
We are our sovereign selves.

PRIESTESS

Priestess bears a great burden,
Seekers seek the wisdom she holds,
Longing to touch what she has sacrificed for,
But there is reason why she is so few,
Yet they are many.

Lonely is the path she walks,
But truly alone she will never be,
She is accompanied by all her sisters,
Near and far, past and present,
Yet there will still never be many.

She is holy and set apart,
Not adopting trendy fads,
Wisdom and beauty everlasting,
She was chosen, she is chaste,
Until her last breath, she will be priestess.

SOUL SISTERS

What a divine thing it is to have soul sisters,
We may not be from the same physical mother,
We may not have found each other until adulthood,
But find each other, we finally did.

Everyone speaks of finding a soul mate in a lover's way,
While no one speaks of finding their soul mate in friends,
Of emotional and intellectual proportions,
What would I do without you all in my life?

When I am losing my mind and feel myself going under,
You are all there, no matter how far apart we may live,
We take turns for whose shoulder is the one to lean on,
Together, we are a whole person, and the burden is less.

LIVESTOCK

To be a woman is to be many things,
Multi-faceted, complex and deep,
But I am not a piece of livestock.
She is not cattle or chattel.
We will not just be your breeders or brooders.

We are human above all else.
It seems you must continue to forget,
So let us remind you.
We do not need your permission.
We are here, we have our own voice.

I am not a piece of livestock.
She is not cattle or chattel.
We will not just be your breeders or brooders.

SECTION II

The Ethereal

AWEN

To be in your presence,
Mother Earth, Awen,
To take in breath and be inspired,
Awenydd.

I am humbled by your sheer might,
No one else is as clothed in life,
Wrap me in your radiant light,
Allow me to share space in your life.

But for a mere speck of time,
My breath is a passing gust,
An afternoon shadow on your lawn,
Give me life-force for my life.

I will tend to the flowers in your field,
I will bathe in your showers of rain,
For without your fertility and generosity,
We would perish in a blink of your eye.

*AWEN FOOTNOTES

Awen is a Welsh word that means inspiration. It can also be found as a word in Cornish and Breton. It is thought of as the muse that inspires the poet. How fitting! It can also be said to be the source of all things, knowledge, or magic. As a symbol, it represents balance. This symbol is mentioned in a Welsh book of myths called the Mabinogian.

Neo-Druids also use the word to refer to flowing energy, or a force that flows with the essence of life.

Awenydd means spirit worker or inspired poet. It is one who is inspired through bardcraft.

ENTROPY

I am descending into entropy.
Whether I'm imploding or exploding,
I do not yet know.
Utter chaos in flux,
Flowing in, flowing out.
Is this quick sand?
No sense of order can I find,
Give me the floor back.
I demand, I cry, I beg.
Will my pleas be heard?
It remains to be seen,
I hold onto hope and wait.

THE LIMINAL MIST

In the liminal mist lies the mystic,
The in-between,
Above it, the Divine,
Below it, the material,
As above, so below.

Beyond the liminal mist,
Is the ethereal,
The shroud, the veil,
Hidden in plain sight,
Only the attuned aware.

The tangible is but passing,
A mere breath on a cold day,
Beware, for that which you seek,
Will surely be found,
Are you certain that it should be?

The veil is thinning,
Soon it will tear to a shred,
Dawn the enlightened age,
Bring forth a new way,
Through the liminal mist, can you see?

AIR

Air, the air I breathe.
An atmospheric mixture,
A delicate balance.

Earth grows green things,
A photosynthesis process.
Oxygen flows, grows.

Water descends here,
The lifeblood of green things.
Washed anew, it grew.

Fire stimulates growth,
It rises like a Phoenix,
Giving fuel and breath.

AMBEDO

Such a melancholic state I do find myself,
A trance I am absorbed into,
Half-conscious, hypnotic,
Vivid senses that enchant me.
I reflect, and I absorb,
Am I awake? I do not know.
Nor do I care to ascertain.
Whatever this may be,
Let me stay, leave me be.
Ambedo. Credo.

OLD ONES

Forgotten by most these days,
The Old Ones are getting angry.
How long can they be spat on,
Before they make their presence known?

We have tried to control Mother Nature,
Routing rivers against their natural course.
Expecting a bumper crop every harvest,
How much more before She says no more?

We are but ants against the Cosmos,
But we are so very arrogant, aren't we?
Do we really think that we can control,
The outcome of the Mighty Forces?

SANDS OF TIME

Do you ever wonder just what
Has been lost to the Sands of Time?
Knowledge, wisdom, technology?
Even the ancient Egyptians had archaeologists.
We will never know what all has been lost.
Who will remember those with no trace?
Do they live on in the Sands of Time?
Can you feel it blowing in the wind?
Epochs lost and epochs future,
What will be our mark and will it last?
Will it withstand the Sands of Time?

RECYCLED

Do you ever look in another's eyes,
And feel that you've met in another time?
That smile looking back at you,
Bringing comfort from another place?
Do you believe in recycled life?

I didn't in the not-so-previous past,
But that was another time and another place,
Now I stand in the here, a different me,
Standing in a different world than I started in,
Wondering how I had never seen.

Now, I do believe in recycled life.
The ancient world did, and the Eastern world does,
Why do more of us not see this way?
There is a real beauty to this and a hope,
A hopefulness that I did not know before.

SECTION III

Turmoil

RANTINGS OF MY MIND

The private space of my most inner thoughts,
How thankful I am that I alone hear them.
For if you could hear them, I think,
That you would question my sanity.

You see, the problem is that no one questions,
Whether the world is as it seems or not.
When you question everything, They fear.
This sphere of perception may not be reality.

Another existential issue that exists,
Is if reality isn't reality, what is reality really?
As lyrical as it is a spherical projection.
These are the rantings of my mind.

Question everything.

NO ONE ELSE

No one else can cut me like a knife,
Like you do.
I would not dare give anyone as much power,
As I give you.
For that would be utter destruction and ruin,
My undoing.

I can barely keep it together as it is,
Why does it hurt so?
You have my heart, my soul, my life,
Please don't hurt me.
I understand your projected anger onto me,
But please don't hurt me.

Why does this pain sting so bad?
When you hurt me, you hurt yourself.
Why don't you understand?
I am defenseless because you're my armor.
I love you with every fiber of my being,
But no one else can hurt me like you.

ERODE

Erosion erodes, erodes away.

It strips away, layer upon layer,
It doesn't care, doesn't discriminate.

Erosion erodes, erodes away.

It eats at the edge, the surface's edge,
It looks like the Earth is melting away.

Erosion erodes, erodes away.

YOU NEVER KNOW

A dollar store closed on a Saturday afternoon,
Customers crowding around the locked door,
Peeking in, prying at the automatic door,
Frustrated, they shake their heads and leave.

Little did we know, on the other side of town,
Police sirens were whooping and wooing,
Approaching a residence, responding to a call,
That store manager deathly silent on the other side.

A mother killed on Mother's Day weekend,
A life snuffed out far, far too soon.
A beautiful soul that was beloved by all,
What did he gain by taking her life?

When you're frustrated, you never know.
When you're tired and angry, you never know.
Oh how I wish I'd known that, but,
The moral is you never really know.

GREED

We are slaves of capitalistic greed.
The machine keeps on turning,
We are but a cog in its gear.
How outraged we would be if we realized,
That debt is their enslavement of us.
We do not need bigger houses,
Six-figure cars, or an eighty-five inch TV!
How did we let them convince us that,
We should keep up with the Joneses?
How sad it is that we bought it,
Hook, line, and sinker.
Now it gets worse, no need to pay today!
Just put it on a line of credit,
Have it now, pay later, it's easy!
What could be better?
Only now we're extended beyond our means,
Getting more maxed out on credit.
Will the bubble burst?
What will you do with your eighty-five inch TV,
When you can no longer even afford tea?

MINUTES FOR SALE!

Minutes for sale! Minutes for sale!
We always think we'll see things,
For what they truly are,
The reality of it is though,
The revelation stares us in the face.
Blindly, right through the mundane.
No other species pays to live on this earth.
We buy objects without purpose,
Without necessity.
The Earth produces the vine and stream,
Yet we sell our souls to corporate machines.
For what? For what I say?
The dollars we earn represent:
The minutes of our lives we've sold.
So make it worth it, make it count.
Or for Pete's sake, buck the system,
Turn away from the path They made,
And just simply live.
Minutes for sale! Minutes for sale!

QUICKSAND

You are sinking so quick,
Suffocating and drowning,
Engulfed in quicksand.
Stop fighting so hard,
You are just sinking quicker.

I know you're a fighter,
But you're writhing, not rising.
Stop shutting me out,
I am not your enemy,
You have to let go of it now.

Let go of the past, it's passed,
You have to forgive yourself.
Only you can release the pain,
If you don't, it will pull you under.
It's time to start healing.

MORPHINE

Give me morphine for my soul,
Make it so I cannot feel this pain,
There has been so much inflicted,
I want to forget and not feel.

Please, I beg of you, on my knees,
Give me another shot that I crave.

Give that euphoric sensation,
Make me feel that drowsiness,
Take this pain and drown it out,
I want to forget and not feel.

If only there really was a true,
Morphine for the soul.

INTO THE NIGHT, AGAIN

A poem about Afghanistan. A beautiful, diverse land that continuously changes hands between different countries or factions that would attempt to control it.

I was born in a fertile land,
A land that has been fought over,
Invaded by forces for as long,
As any memory serves.

Some invaders poisoned our wells,
Some made sure girls went to school,
But the fact remains that they are gone,
And we remain in the ruins.

Now we are starving and hunted,
Girls are once again forced home,
There is no help for us, lest we escape,
And that is a lucky few, too few.

Some protected our fields of poppy,
Others would mine our lithium,
But you won't aid us in our need,
How many times must we bear this?

Still we remain strong and steadfast,
We have stood for generations,
And we shall continue to yet again,
We are the Graveyard of Empires.

JUSTICE SERVED TOO LATE

Justice is not like revenge,
It is not a dish best served cold.

Justice served too little too late,
Does not bring a life back from the dead.

"Get Justice" is an insult to the lives lost,
That were cost before that statement was made.

How do you get Justice for a heinous crime?
Does that give rest or comfort to its victims?

Justice does not bring a life back from the dead,
No matter how much you think it consoles you.

THE MORE I ASK

The more I ask, answers I do receive,
Yet the more answers I get,
The more questions that I have.

Such a vicious cycle,
That the more I ask,
The more I ask.

So I have learned once more,
That the more I ask,
The more I ask again, and again...

BLAP, BLAP

There I sat, hunkered down in the kitchen,
So scared that I was trembling.

First volley of shots: "Is this really happening?"
Quiet falls, is it all over?
Second volley comes: "Oh God, this is really happening?"
When will this be over?

When I finally heard the sirens in the distance,
An eternity passed before they closed the distance.

But the moment doesn't come to an end,
It keeps on playing, there's no pause button.
I keep replaying those events,
"How did we even end up there at all?"

SECTION IV

Strength

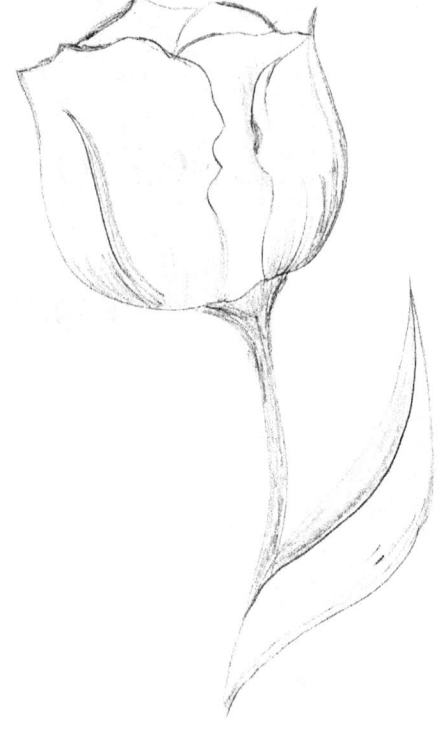

GLUE ON IT

I sit writing in a café, crying,
I've had two-and-a-half hours sleep,
I thought I was keeping it together,
I was so busy gluing you back together,
That I didn't see the cracks in myself.
As I poured my soul onto the written page,
It all came pouring out, drop by drop.
I have cried alone in cafés,
I have been so many miles away.
I just want to hold you tight and near.
Let me put some glue on it,
I can put the pieces back together again.

AUTONOMY

Your rights end where mine begin,
Your rights and my rights meet in the middle,
Your opinions end where my rights begin,
You have the freedom of thought and speech,
But you may not trample on my freedoms,
You are not required to agree with my choices,
But you must respect my existence as a human,
For every extreme side that an opinion sits on,
There is a multitude more like a wagon's spoke.
You cannot fight fire with fire, don't you see?
The only balance is opposite and equal,
So let us walk with love and respect of each.
For we all have the free will to choose,
And we all have our own autonomy completely,
So why must we be divided and hateful,
After all, we are all humans and beautifully so.

FIRE-BORNE

From a lake of fire,
Like a Phoenix reborne,
I am Fire-Borne.

From this lake of fire,
I burned off the scorn,
I am Fire-Borne.

With wings of ruby and gold,
I now soar above the forlorn,
I am Fire-Borne.

I beseech you to burn the chaff,
Wings outstretched and adorned,
We become Fire-Borne.

HONOUR AND STRENGTH

Strength is not just a physical trait,
We must stop this dangerous thinking,
Physical strength is a brutish thing,
Requiring no measure of intelligence,
Character, ethics, honour, nor courage.
Strength is wiseness, kindness, charity,
Strength is honesty, integrity, amnesty.

Honour is not just laurels and accolades,
It cannot be bought, only sought.
Narrow is the door to its Seekers,
But beyond it's threshold shall they be filled,
Fulfilled to the brim with their destiny,
Honour is respect, esteem, commitment,
Honour is honesty, integrity, amnesty.

HANGING BY A THREAD

When you're hanging by a thread,
And the thread is nothing but silk,
Spin that silk like a web,
To catch those that set the trap.

I thought I was at the end of my rope,
How I wish I was! Ha!
A rope is stronger, silk is dainty,
But I will not fall, I will not let go.

When you're hanging, dangling,
When you're angling, mangling,
When you're wrangling, strangling,
Spin that silk like a web.

ON THE SHOULDERS OF OTHERS

On the shoulders of others,
We reach the heights we ascend to,
Never on our own, lest we become boastful,
Brick by brick, they paved the path,
Stone by stone, they laid the foundation.

How haughty and arrogant are we?
Paying no attention to our Elders,
And the price that they paid for us.
We are nowhere without the debt they paid,
Let it not be for nothing that they bled.

SECTION V

In Homage

ATLAS SHRUGGED

Atlas, holding the world on his shoulders,
Tired is he, and the groaning becomes louder,
How much longer can he endure?
How much more should he be required?

Metaphorically, allegorically,
Metaphysically, rhetorically,
He is wary and decided,
On the path the Fates have guided.

So he shrugged.

MIND KILLER

Litany Against Hate

Fear is not the mind-killer.
Hate is the mind-killer.
I must not hate, we must not hate.
Hate is the poison that brings total division.
I will not permit it to become a part of me.
And when it flows past, we must turn an inner eye.
When the hate has gone, there will be no more division.

*MIND KILLER FOOTNOTE

This poem is a twist on the famous Litany Against Fear *from* Dune. Dune *was written by Frank Herbert and published in 1965. It spawned an entire series of books, and a fandom spanning 6 decades. It has since been brought to the big screen several times. This poem is meant to honor Herbert's concept, but with my own twist; revealing a new meaning.*

INTERLINKED

Above the blue sky,
Below the blue sky,
Interlinked.

Below the stormy sea,
Upon the stormy sea,
Interlinked.

Upon the green grass,
Within the green grass,
Interlinked.

Within the field of wheat,
Through the field of wheat,
Interlinked.

Through the window,
Through the window,
Interlinked.

*INTERLINKED FOOTNOTE

Based on a scene from Blade Runner 2049. Officer K undergoes an anti-empathy test. In the original movie there is a test called the Voit-Kompff test that was designed to elicit an empathetic response to detect replicants. The one administered in Blade Runner 2049 is actually designed to do the opposite, which is to make sure that replicants are not developing emotional or empathetic responses. A baseline is established and how the respondent answers determines their state. The beautiful irony is that the cells interlinked scene in Blade Runner 2049 is based on a section of a poem by Vladimir Nabokov called Pale Fire. This means that my poem is based on a movie scene that is based on a poem.

DON'T BURN ME

If you are not going to ignite my innermost fire,
Then do not burn me with your superficial passion.
For once a thing has been set on fire,
It cannot be rekindled again.

I will not confuse the smoke of ruined ashes,
For a smoke signal of our devotion.
Set your pen to paper and write a heartfelt sonnet;
For I will not be a crumpled, burnt up wad of paper.

Spare the innocent and let them go.
Don't burn them with zealous passion,
That burns bright but burns out quick.
Don't burn me.

*DON'T BURN ME FOOTNOTE

This poem is in homage to a poem by Sergei Yesenin, called You Do Not Love Me. *Yesenin is considered to be one of the most famous Russian poets. Yet he did not live a long life, living to be only thirty years old. I have read the poem in both English and in Russian. It is a truly deep, thought-provoking poem that instantly had me writing this homage. If you would like to explore it further, I recommend a YouTube video titled* Learning Russian from Yesenin's poem *uploaded by the channel* Be Fluent in Russian.

GLOSSARY

Ambedo - From The Dictionary of Obscure Sorrows
noun. A kind of melancholic trance in which you become completely absorbed in vivid sensory details.

Ambuscade - From Merriam-Webster Dictionary
noun. Synonym for ambush. Ironically, ambush is the older form of the word.

Awen - From Geiriadur Prifysgol Cymru
noun. A Welsh word meaning poetic inspiration.
Variation: Awenydd. A Welsh word meaning poet.

Credo - From Merriam-Webster Dictionary
noun. A guiding belief or principle. Comes from Latin, meaning: I believe.

Liminal - From Cambridge Dictionary
adjective. Between or belonging to two different places.

Replicant - From Collins Online Dictionary
noun. A science fiction term for an android indistinguishable from a human being.

ABOUT THE AUTHOR

Rachel Rash

Rachel is a contemporary American poet. An awenydd and true renaissance woman. If you are not yet familiar with the meaning of awenydd, just wait. There is a poem about it in this very book! Rachel is enraptured by the elegance of where science and mysticism meet, which create exquisite depth to her prose.

From attending her local Comic-Con to writing a poem based on a scene from the newest Blade Runner, to using a Fibonacci number sequence on her twenty-first birthday cake, Rachel identifies as a nerd. She spends her precious free time with her husband, son, and animals in the beautiful state of Arkansas. She lives a busy life, fueled by coffee (because there isn't much sleep).

www.ingramcontent.com/pod-product-compliance
Lightning Source LLC
Chambersburg PA
CBHW060424050426
42449CB00009B/2115